IOS Programming For Beginners

The Simple Guide to Learning IOS Programming Fast!

Table Of Contents

Introduction   1

Chapter 1: Things You Need   2

Chapter 2: The Xcode 6 Platform and Swift code   6

Chapter 3: Learning Xcode 6   12

Chapter 4: Anatomy of an App   16

Chapter 5: Developing a basic Swift App   18

Chapter 6: The Xcode 6 Interface Building with
Auto Layout   32

Chapter 7: Essential Swift Programming Concepts   51

Conclusion   64

Introduction

I want to thank you and congratulate you for downloading the book, *"IOS Programming For Beginners"*.

This book contains helpful information about IOS programming language, what it is, and how it's used.

You will learn about the software used to create apps, and the programming language Swift. You will soon discover the basics of app development for IOS, and be creating your own apps in no time!

This book includes helpful tips and techniques that will allow you to begin using IOS to create your very own apps fast, and in fact will take you step by step through creating your first app!

App creation can be a fun hobby, and also a lucrative business. This book is a fantastic place to begin with app development, regardless of your final goals!

Thanks again for downloading this book, I hope you enjoy it!

Chapter 1:
Things You Need

The only thing your really need in order to learn IOS development is a computer running Mac OS. That's essential because that's the only way you will be able to follow along the instructions in this book. The reason you need a Mac is because the program that we use to build apps on or write our code only runs on OSX, which is the operating system for a MAC. You may have heard of solutions that run on PCs or the Microsoft Windows operating system but those are 3rd party solutions that are not endorsed or supported by Apple. In the lesson examples that are provided in this book we will be using official Apple tools and materials.

The Mac doesn't have to be expensive. For example, most of the programming exercises indicated in this book were done on a used 13" Macbook Pro 2011 model that runs on a 2.4 Ghz Intel Core i5, 8GB of RAM and 120GB SSD without any performance issues. So if you're on a budget, we recommend that you buy a used Macbook or Mac.

Once you have your Mac, you can download the programming platform where we will be writing our code and creating our app. That program is called Xcode 6 and it is available in the Mac app store for free. The only requirement is that you need at least OSX 10.9.4 or later with 2.46 GB of space to run it. That translates to OSX Mavericks, which is a free upgrade if you are running an operating system version later than Mavericks.

So what does this Xcode 6 program allow you to do? Well if you think about an app for a second, at the very basic level it consists of two things:

1. User Interface – This is what the user sees on the phone and what the user interacts with.

2. Logic and Response – This is what happens in response to the user interacting with the app.

Xcode 6 allows you to create this user interface visually just by dragging and dropping elements on to the screen. It also allows you to write that logic and express it in terms of code. So you're able to code what happens when a user taps a button or what happens when the user swipes. You are able to use that code to perform calculations, go fetch data, respond to the user or update the view.

Furthermore, Xcode 6 also lets us test our app. So in addition to creating the user interface and wiring up that logic with code, we can test run the app in Xcode 6. Xcode 6 has a great simulator that will appear on your screen to mimic the iPhone and it will run your app inside of that so you can see what your app looks like; you can use and test your app without actually having an iPhone. So it's not even a requirement to have a device if you want to build an iPhone app.

We use code to express the logic and what happens when the user interacts with your app's user interface. That code follows a set of rules and follows a certain framework just like a language, that's why it is called Programming Language.

You may have heard that Apple released a second programming language for building iPhone apps called Swift. This is what the exercises in this book are going to teach you how to use. The reason Swift is better for beginners to learn how to build apps with is because the syntax and the structure of the language is much more natural and intuitive. Its a lot more easier to read and to understand for beginners. In the past when IOS programming relied on the Objective C programming language, a lot of beginners struggled with the syntax, and all of the different symbols and characters used to write the code. They struggled to remember what keywords to use and how to declare certain things. With Swift, the syntax is more like plain English so it feels less like you have to learn a second language.

So that's all there really is to it. At the very core, you're going to learn how to use Xcode 6 to build your user interface, and Swift programming language to respond to user events and gesture to express logic.

So after you finish building your app in Xcode 6 and testing it on the simulator, how are you going to get it on your device or how are you going to get it to the app store? Well this part actually requires you to have an Apple Developer Program membership. This is a yearly $99 fee that Apple charges which allows you to publish as many apps on the app store as you want, and allows you to install it on your device. Unfortunately, there is no other way to put your app on an actual device unless you're a member of this developer program.

So when you sign-up for the Apple Developer Program, it gives you access to two websites:

1. Provisioning Portal – This the place where you upload your certificates and create your profiles that dictate which devices your app can be installed on.

2. iTunes connect – This is the place where you will create the catalog listing for your app with screenshots. It is basically when you browse the app store and you see all those app lists where you can see the price and

description, you create all of those here in iTunes connect. You can also check the stats for your app in terms of downloads and rankings. If you have ads or iAd in you app, you can check your earnings reports also. If you have in-app purchases iTunes connect is where you would configure them as well.

So there you have it, the only thing you really require is a Mac which will allow you to install Xcode 6, which is free, to build and test your app. If you want to deploy your app into the app store or to any device, you can sign-up to the Apple Developer Program which gives you access to two websites to allow you to do that.

Chapter 2:
The Xcode 6 Platform and Swift code

Now we're going to dabble in some Swift code and just get our feet wet. What's important in this chapter is you try to do the exercises yourself. You should have a Mac and you should have Xcode 6 installed from the Mac app store.

When you open Xcode for the first time and you will be presented with the main menu where you will see an option that says "Get started with a playground". If you don't have this welcome menu, you can easily open a new playground by going to the menu bar on the top and selecting file→ new → playground.

So we're not starting a whole new app project in this exercise. We're using something called a playground which is newly introduced in Xcode 6. You can think of a playground as a lightweight way for us to try and test out some code without fully having to commit to starting a whole new app project. For now, we just need to get our feet wet and test out some Swift code. The key thing is to try it out yourself, so I recommend you open your Mac and launch Xcode 6 and just follow along.

So after you select "Get started with a playground" in the Xcode 6 main menu, you will be presented with a name and a platform so just leave it as is for now and just click "next" and save it on the desktop.

Now you will have a playground main window and this is the area where you will type in the Swift code for the app. Right now we will just create a simple "Hello World" app.

So we're just going to put a string into the variable message. A string is just a piece of text, think of it like that, and it's surrounded by quote symbols (""). The equal sign means to denote or to designate; in this case we're designating the string "Hello World" to the variable named message.

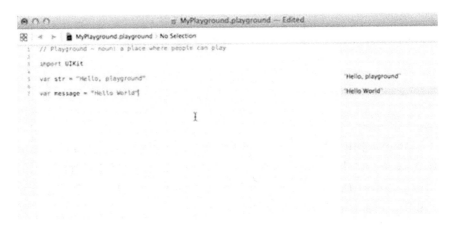

On the right hand side of this playground, you can see the result of what you just typed. Now, if I want to print the string designated to the variable message, you can just make use of "println" meaning print line and it will output the string that you designated to the variable message.

```
// Playground – noun: a place where people can play

import UIKit

var str = "Hello, playground"                    "Hello, playground"

var message = "Hello World"                       "Hello World"

println(message)                                  "Hello World"
```

Let's look at other examples:

```
// Playground – noun: a place where people can play

import UIKit

var str = "Hello, playground"                    "Hello, playground"

var message = "Hello World"                       "Hello World"

println(message)                                  "Hello World"

var a = 10                                        10

var b = 15                                        15

var total = a + b
```

So here we put the value *10* to the variable *a*, value *15* to the variable *b*, and we created a new variable *total* which is the sum of *a* and *b*. So If we want to print the *total*, it will output the sum of *a* and *b* which is *25*.

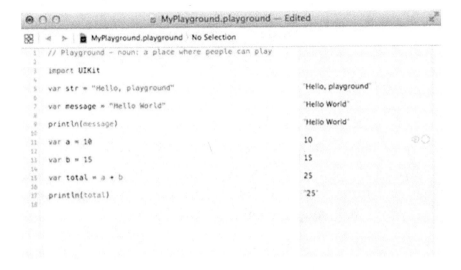

So you can see that on the right hand side it kind of gives you a preview of what's happening as you write these lines of code. Now let's try something different:

```
// Playground - noun: a place where people can play

import UIKit

var str = "Hello, playground"        "Hello, playground"

var message = "Hello World"          "Hello World"

println(message)                     "Hello World"

var a = 10                           10

var b = 15                           15

var total = a + b                    25

println(total)                       "25"

if (total < 20)
{
    println("Hello")
}
```

In the example above, we make use of the '*if*', *then* logic. As you can see on the output window on the right side nothing happens when you typed in the code

```
if (total < 20)

{

    println ("Hello")

}
```

Of course, nothing happens because the variable *total* is *a + b* is equal to *25*. The condition that is set for the '*if*' statement, which as a *total* should be less than 20, is not fulfilled. But, let's say that we change the value of variable *a* to 1:

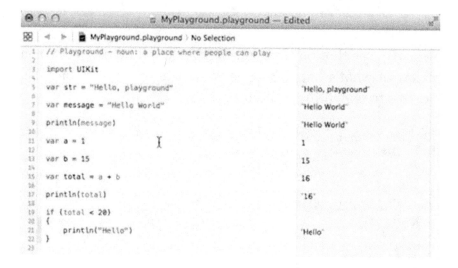

Now that the value of variable *a* changed to *1,* this changed the *total* value as well, in this case to *16*. It fulfills the condition of the '*if*' statement, which as a *total* should be less than 20, and in turn prints the string *"Hello".*

So an '*if*' statement gives us the power to perform some logic and we will go more into that as we go along. For now, don't worry about trying to memorize all the syntax or the structure of the examples so far. We're going to go through in detail all of the different aspects of the Swift mechanics in the succeeding chapters. Right now, all you need to do is try it on your computer, open up your Xcode 6 and try it out.

The reason that I'm are asking you to do this is that I've found out that the most intimidating thing for a student trying to learn IOS development is the programming language aspect of it. I hope that by following along and typing out the statements indicated in the examples above, you'll find out that its actually very logical, easy to follow and pretty straightforward and nothing to be fearful about.

Chapter 3:
Learning Xcode 6

In this chapter, we're going to go through a tutorial of Xcode 6, the program in which you will be spending a lot of time developing apps. We're using Xcode 6 which is the newest version.

Every year or two Apple rolls out a new version. There are changes between the different versions, but they aren't so drastic that you have to relearn everything each time a new version comes up. It's kind of like how Adobe rolls out a new version of Photoshop. Each iteration has new features but the core product is still there. If you know how to use one version, you will be pretty well versed on the next one.

In this chapter we will be going through the major sections of the Xcode interface that you will be using the most. This will set you up for that core functionality that you can leverage for any version of Xcode. We're going to start by creating a new Xcode project. We're not going to touch into too much detail all of the different project types or settings. In the next chapter we will actually create a new project and go through the settings then. For now, we just want to get our feet wet and whip up a new project. We will pick single view application and get to the main interface so you can familiarize yourself with the different sections of the program.

The first thing you'll notice is that the interface is split up into 3 distinct sections. You have the left pane, which is your *project file navigator*. When you create a new app project, it consists of different folders and files. This is where you can look at various files of your project. This pane also has a series of tabs, which we will be discussing in future chapters.

When you click on a file for example the 'ViewController.swift', the middle part changes into your code editor section. It actually depends on what kind of file you select on your project file navigator on the left side, if it's a code file, you will see your lines of code here and you will be able write and edit your code there as well.

If you are selecting however, one of the interface files, the middle section changes into your interface builder, which is where you will be working visually to build your interface.

The right portion of Xcode 6 is the *inspector pane*. Here, it gives you details about the file you have highlighted or the file that you are currently looking at. The inspector pane is split into two different panes, one taking up 75% at the top, and the bottom pane is called the library pane.

The library pane displays different elements that you can add to your interface. In the succeeding chapters when we are building our interface we're literally dragging and dropping different elements from here.

If we select an element, for example, you drag a *Button* onto your interface builder from your library and click on it, when you select the Attributes tab on your inspector pane, you will see all the attributes for your *Button*.

Another thing about the Xcode 6 interface is that there's actually a hidden section down at the bottom portion when you are in a code file such as *'ViewController.swift'*. You can bring it up by clicking *View → Debug area → Show Debug Area*. This section is the Debug Area where we will be able to inspect your code. You will be able to see errors and error messages and will be able to keep track of different variables.

It is basically an area that's going to be very helpful when you start writing and troubleshoot your code.

At the very top, the most prominent thing you'll also notice is the Play button. This *Play* button will actually run and test your project in the simulator. Once you click on *Play* you will now notice that the *Stop* button can now also be selected. This will stop your project from running on the simulator and it will return you back to the project for editing.

When you click *Play*, you will see your simulator pop up on your screen, and as I've mentioned before, this mimics an iPhone, so you don't actually need the device to test your app in. As soon as you click *Play* and run your project in Xcode, it launches the app on the simulator and it allows you to test run your app. To stop the test run on the simulator all you have to do is click the stop button at the top.

There's also a drop down option on the top as well that lets you select what kind of simulator to test run your project in. You can try out your app on different devices. There's also an iOS device option which is used when you actually have a device to test on and you have an Apple Developer Program Membership to deploy your app on the phone.

You also have a status bar that tells you if there are any errors on your app when you run it, among other things. Immediately to the right hand side of your status bar are some buttons to toggle between the different views that you can have when using Xcode 6.

So at its core, that's pretty much what Xcode 6 is; you have your file navigator on the left, your code editor on the middle, your inspector pane on the right, the Debug area on the bottom, and the status bar on the topmost part. These are Xcode's core for the last few iterations.

Do not worry if it looks confusing to you because just like any other program or app, the more you use it, the more comfortable you'll feel in it. When we start developing apps we'll be using all of this section and you'll get familiar with all of these aspects.

Chapter 4:
Anatomy of an App

In this chapter, we will be discussing the anatomy of an iPhone app. We're going to go over the major components that all iPhone apps have in common. Before we dive into Xcode and show you how the app represents those different components, we're going to go over the different parts of an iPhone app first.

An iPhone app is basically divided into the following components:

1. View – This is what the user sees and interacts with in their phone.

2. View controller – The view controller is the one that manages the view.

3. Model – The model manages the data for your app.

So how do these three components work together to form a functioning app? Well, the *View Controller* sits in between the *Model* and the *View* and manages the communication between the two. For example, the *View controller* may ask the *Model* for some data such as a list of contacts, and then the *View controller* will pass that data to the *View* to render it to the user. Similarly, if the user interacts with the V*iew*, let's say the user deletes a contact, the *View controller* then gets that interaction and passes it to the *Model* to tell it to remove the contact since only the *Model* manages the data.

So as you can see, each component has its own set of responsibilities and roles within the app and must work together to form a functioning app. This division of labor and the way that the communication happens between each component is a well-known design pattern in programming called a *Model View Controller* pattern or MVC.

A *Design pattern* is simply a best practice pattern or way to solve a common problem. IOS development makes use of this design pattern heavily to structure the way that apps are built. By following this design pattern, it is easier to maintain and change the code in the future if necessary, because each component has a well-defined and contained set of responsibilities. It is easy to swap in and out the components in the future if you need to make an update. It also helps with troubleshooting your code if you have a bug. Depending on what kind of bug it is, if it is a display issue or a data issue, you would know where to look. Instead of looking all over the project if the responsibilities were merged or molded together, you would just have to look at a single component if you follow this design pattern.

Chapter 5:
Developing a basic Swift App

In this chapter, we will be starting our first Xcode project and building our first app. You should have Xcode 6 installed by now on your Mac. When you open up Xcode you will see the welcoming screen that gives you these options:

1. Get started with a playground

2. Create a new Xcode project

3. Check out an existing project

At this point you have to select *Create a new Xcode project*. There will be times when you won't see the welcoming screen so all you have to do is go to the Xcode menu bar on the top and click File → New → Project which basically does the same thing as when you select *Create a new Xcode project* on the welcoming screen.

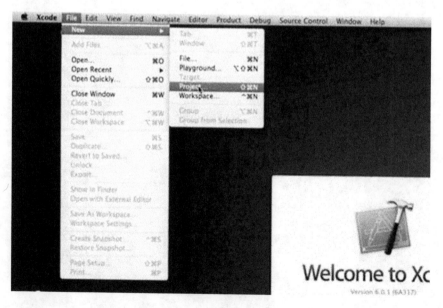

The first dialogue that you will see after that will be one for choosing a template for your new project. The first thing you want to do if you don't see any of the templates is make sure you have the *Application* option selected or highlighted under iOS on the left-hand side. You should see the different templates available to you.

We're going to start with the most basic one which gives you a single blank view on your project which is *Single View Application* template. Depending on what type of project that you want to build, for example, if you want to build apps with tabs along the bottom you could choose the *Tabbed Application* template as a starting point. Likewise, if you want to build a page-based one or a master detail type of app, the *Page-based Application* template is a good starting point.

That's not to say that we can't get to the other templates by choosing the *Single View Application* template, it's just a better starting point. We could still add a tab bar or add a page-based navigation to your Single View Application template, it just depends which one is a better starting point for your app.

We're going to select *Single View Application* and then click *Next*. We're going to go through the settings together and you may want to pay attention to these settings since it may alter what you see in the next view.

You will be presented with three settings, namely:

1. Product Name – That's just what your app is going to be named. For this exercise we'll just put the name of your app as "Hello World".

2. Organization Name – Here you could put your personal name or company name.

3. Organization Identifier – This basically will be used in conjunction with your product name to create a unique Bundle or app Identifier.

4. Language – You want to make sure to choose Swift in this section since we will be using the Swift programming language.

5. Devices – We're only talking about iPhone at this point so make sure to choose iPhone under this option.

6. Use Core Data – Make sure this option is unchecked.

Click *next* after you have gone through the settings as indicated above.

Xcode will now present you with a window that shows you where to save your settings for this app, so for now we'll just save it on the Desktop. Make sure that the Desktop option is highlighted on the left side. You want to make sure before you click *Create* at the bottom that the *Source Control* check box is unchecked.

Source Control is basically a way of storing and managing your code; tracking your changes as you progress in your project, but for now we won't be using this option.

Now you will be in your Xcode main interface window. We will now go through the files that you will have in your new project.

At the very top the root node is your project properties. When you click that, on the editor area of Xcode at the center pane, you're going to see all of your project configuration settings which we will be using as we go along.

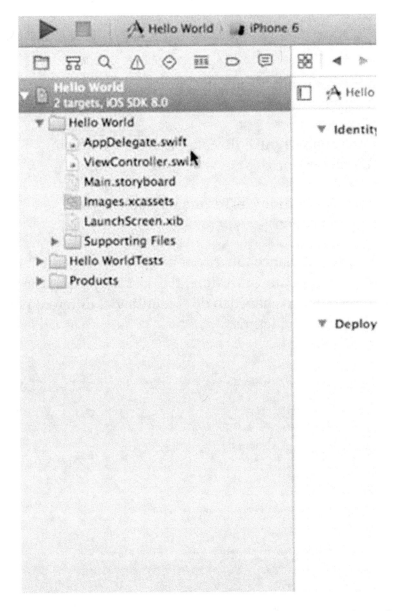

Moving on, you also have the AppDelegate.swift, which provides a chance for you to type in some code or logic where you can handle different situations that arise in the lifetime of your application. For example, if you read some of the things typed in the editor pane you will see:

- func applicationDidEnterBackground(application: UIApplication)

- func applicationWillEnterForeground(application: UIApplication)

- func applicationDidBecomeActive(application: UIApplication)

- func applicationWillTerminate(application: UIApplication)

So it gives you a chance to write code to maybe save that data, or restore some data or restore the last view the user was using. It gives you a chance to do something at different points in the application's lifetime.

```
        return true
    }

func applicationWillResignActive(application: UIApplication) {
    // Sent when the application is about to move from active to inactive state. This can occur
        temporary interruptions (such as an incoming phone call or SMS message) or when the use
        and it begins the transition to the background state.
    // Use this method to pause ongoing tasks, disable timers, and throttle down OpenGL ES fram
        use this method to pause the game.
    }

func applicationDidEnterBackground(application: UIApplication) {
    // Use this method to release shared resources, save user data, invalidate timers, and stor
        state information to restore your application to its current state in case it is termin
    // If your application supports background execution, this method is called instead of appl
        when the user quits.
    }

func applicationWillEnterForeground(application: UIApplication) {
    // Called as part of the transition from the background to the inactive state; here you can
        changes made on entering the background.
    }

func applicationDidBecomeActive(application: UIApplication) {
    // Restart any tasks that were paused (or not yet started) while the application was inacti
        was previously in the background, optionally refresh the user interface.
    }

func applicationWillTerminate(application: UIApplication) {
    // Called when the application is about to terminate. Save data if appropriate. See also
        applicationDidEnterBackground:.
    }
```

Another thing is the ViewController.swift that we briefly discussed together with the Model View Controller or MVC design pattern in the last chapter. So this view controller is what manages the view.

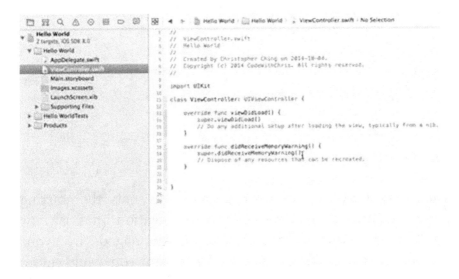

Next is the *Main.storyboard*. When you click this, your editor pane turns into the interface builder. Now you see the view for your single view application. This is what the view controller actually manages. Now, what is a storyboard? The storyboard manages the flow of your application in a visual manner.

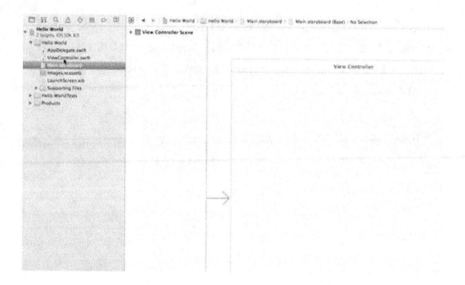

The arrow that you see in this view represents the starting point or the entry point of your application that is now pointing to your View, which is managed by your *ViewController.swift*. It is possible when you build more complex apps that you will have multiple views and multiple view controllers and this arrow will indicate where the starting point is.

Here's some tips on how to navigate the story board; you can double-click the area to zoom out or you can right click and pick a zoom level. You can double-click again to zoom back in.

Moving on, we have your *Images.xcassets* that is your image assets library. This is where you're going to add image assets to your project. You can literally just create new image sets and drag and drop your assets in here and refer to them by their name that you give them in this option.

Lastly, you have the *LaunchScreen.zib*, which is another interface builder file. This represents the startup screen for your app.

The first thing that we need to do now is to go back to your *Main.storyboard* and we're going to do our "Hello World" demo application. Now if you've ever done any other programming education before you may recognize that "Hello World" is the customary first app or first program and that's what we're going to do here iOS style.

Now we're looking at Main.storyboard and in our editor we see our view here. What we're going to do is visually add a label to the view and just change the text of the label to say "Hello World" and then we're going to run our application.

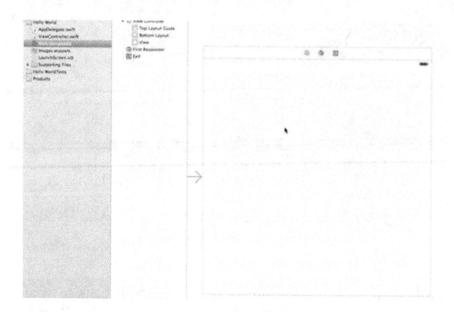

In the lower right hand corner, if you remember, this is called the library pane. If you don't see the different elements, make sure that you're on the elements tab (circular icon). There's also another button at the bottom left of the library pane which changes to the different views available such as list view or grid view.

Beside the view button there's a search box that allows you to filter through the library. Just type "Label" in the search box so that you will see the "Label" element. Click and drag it to your View at the center.

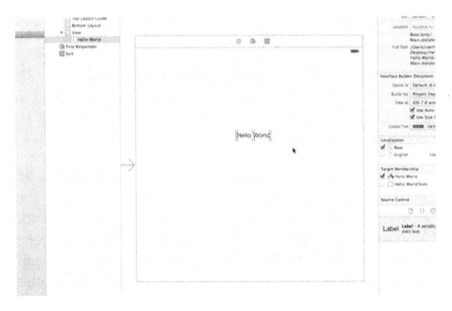

At this point, we can change the text of the label. Just double-click it and type "Hello World". Next, we're actually going to run our app and watch it on the simulator.

On the upper left-hand corner of Xcode 6 make sure that you've selected iPhone 6 and hit run or the Play button. It will compile your application and it will launch the iOS simulator.

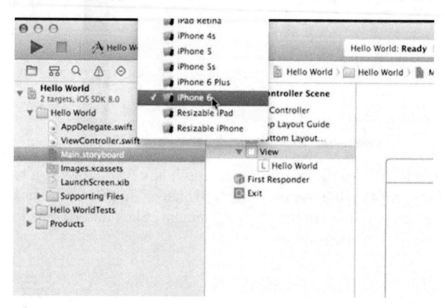

You'll notice that we see the label in our view but it's not in the center. Instead, it is off to the side. Therefore, what we need to do is stop our application running on the simulator by pressing the 'Stop' button on the upper left.

If you have trouble running your application or if there's an error that pops up, one thing you can try is to click the simulator first and on the top menu bar click on iOS Simulator → Reset Content and Settings to reset your simulator to its original default blank state. It will be as you if you really want to reset it so just click Reset. You can run your app again after you reset.

Now, let's look at the issue of the label positioning. The reason the label is off center is because iOS uses a system called auto layout to determine where the element should sit. Auto layout describes the position of the element based on something called constraints. We're going to take a look at that now.

Click your label and down at the lower right-hand corner of the center pane is an icon that says *Align*.

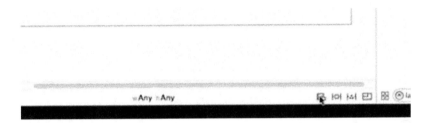

Click on that, and at this point, we will add two alignment constraints. Put a check on the "Horizontal Center in Container" and "Vertical Center in Container" options and click "Add 2 constraints".

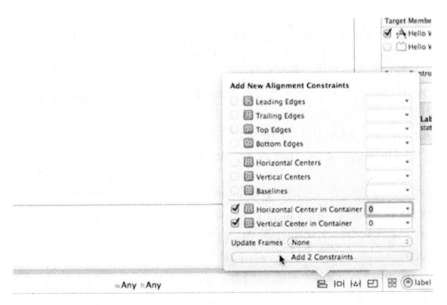

Once you do that, you'll notice that there are two triggers that appear on the view, both horizontal and vertical. They are the constraints for your element that is at the center. You'll also notice in the pane on the left, there's now a constraint option that when you click, will collapse the option and you will see the two constraints (horizontal and vertical).

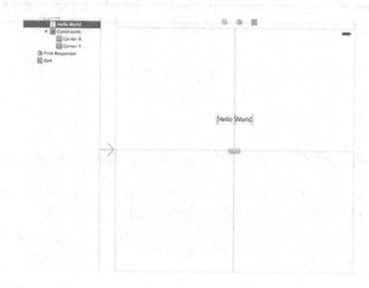

If you don't see the left pane, there's a button down at the bottom that hides and un-hides that area.

Now if you run it again in the simulator, you'll see now that the label is actually in the center, because it's going to read those constraints and it's going to, based on those constraints, vertically and horizontally center that element.

The reason that this is good rather than positioning exactly where we put it, and also a reason why auto layout is good is because it works the same way on any screen. You can rotate it horizontally and it would still be in the center. You can have a bigger or smaller screen, and based on those constraints it will still be centered. Now that Apple is creating multiple screen sizes, it is even more important to use auto layout.

So in order to rotate your simulator just click *Hardware →*
Rotate Left or Rotate Right or you can just hold down
Command + Left or Right arrows.

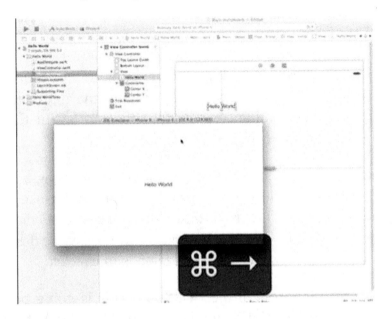

So, congratulations you've just created your first simple app.

Chapter 6:
The Xcode 6 Interface Building with Auto Layout

In this chapter, we're going to build a simple interface only version of the card game: War. We're going to start our new Xcode project and we're also going to build the interface for our app. We'll get a chance to work with auto layout that is more in-depth compared to what we did last time.

So create a new project on Xcode 6 and choose Single View Application. Put "War" as the product name and make sure you choose *Swift* as the programming language and *Device* set to iPhone and Core data unchecked. Save it on your desktop and make sure the *Source control* option is unchecked.

We now default to our project settings. This is going be the same as our "Hello World" application that we did last time, an empty single view application.

Let's just go straight into our storyboard. So if you're not familiar with the card game *War*, what happens is that the deck of cards gets split into two piles, divided evenly between two players. Each player draws the top card off their deck and compares the value. Whoever has the larger value gets the point. It then repeats like that, drawing the top card off each deck.

Our interface is just going to be two cards, or two images representing the two cards with a button that when you click, will draw the next two cards. Now the first thing you'll notice in this user interface is that it's a big square. You may be asking why it is a square and not a rectangle that represents the iPhone view.

You can actually change it down in the option below. You can specify how big your canvas size should be. This default square accommodates all types of layouts including iPad. We can even change it to a narrow one and will display the base values for 3.5-inch, 4-inch, and 4.7-inch iPhones in portrait or landscape view.

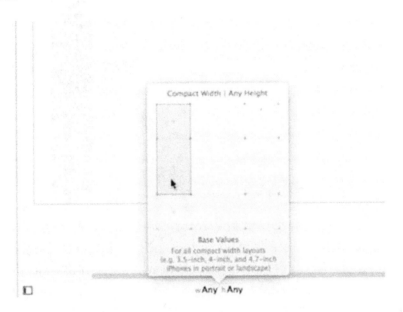

At the end of the day it doesn't really matter because if you remember from the last chapter when we positioned the label, we did it based on relative values of the constraints with auto layout. Bottom-line, whatever screen size it's going to be, it will follow those constraints to position the elements. But, this gives us a good visual representation of what we would see when we run the app in simulator.

The first thing that we're going to do is add an image view element onto the view controller. An image view element displays an image. We're going to be displaying the card images with it. On the right-hand corner, in the bottom-right where we have our library pane, filter it by typing 'imageview'.

Click and drag that onto the interface builder in the center. Once you put it there it kind of expands to take up the whole space which we don't want. We know what size it should be so we need to re-size it by click on the *Pinning* button at the bottom of the interface builder and we'll set the width to a value of 120 and the height to 170 and click *add 2 constraints*.

Now you can see from the project file navigator on the left when you click *View → Image view → Constraints*, you will see that there's two constraints for the image view. So, when it gets displayed when you run the app, it will follow these two constraint rules and adjust the height and width appropriately.

Right now in our interface builder, we can actually update the element to follow those two constraints by clicking the *Resolve Auto Layout Issues* icon and click *Update frames.*

You can now see that it follows those two constraints and gets the appropriate size.

However, there are no rules for positioning it right now. So, what we can do using auto layout constraints again, is you can click the image view and click on the *Align* icon at the bottom, and then click on the |---| icon and anchor it with a value of 50 pixels from the left edge and click *add 1 constraints.*

Again, it's not updated for the view and you can see the dotted outline where the new image view is going to be positioned once you update frames based on the constraints. So, once again click *Resolve Auto Layout Issues* and click *update frames* and it calculates what it should look like based on the constraints that you added.

Now if you want to vertically center this, just go to *Align*, put a check on *Vertical Center in Container,* and click *Add 1 constraints*.

You will again see the dotted line where the *imageview* will go once you update frames. Click *Resolve Auto Layout Issues* at the bottom again and click *Update frames*.

Right now if you run it in the simulator, you won't see anything since because the *imageview* actually has no image associated to it, so it's going to be transparent. We're going to go over here to the attributes tab for the imageview, making sure our imageview is selected, and we're going to change the background.

If you click the icon right indicated below, you're going to get a color picker. If you click on the up & down arrow to the right, you will get the default color presets. So just select the color picker and just give it any color you like, so that you can see it and how it is positioned.

Click on the Play button on the top right to run the app in the simulator.

So there it is. Its 50 pixel off the side and it is vertically aligned and centered, and the height and the width is what we have specified it to be. If we rotate the iPhone simulator by pressing the *Command button* and then *left,* you can see that it follows the same constraints. It is vertically aligned and is 50 pixels off the edge.

Now before we move any further, Auto layout and constraints can be frustrating, especially when you're doing it for the first time. Trying to get things positioned based on these rules is not immediately intuitive. But, once you do it, you get familiar with it by doing it a bunch of times and it becomes more natural and you get to know what to avoid.

So it is recommended that you try to experiment, try things out, lay things out on your screen. Add constraints and run it on the simulator and see how the constraints affect how things are laid out.

Here's a tip on what not to do when you want to edit your constraints. Don't click your element and try to edit your constraints using the menu options below, because they are just for adding new constraints. What you'll end up doing is having two constraints trying to specify the same thing.

Instead, you really want to be looking at this document outline and select the constraint that you want to change. Then on the right hand side on the inspector pane under the attributes tab, you can edit the values. That's how you want to edit your constraints.

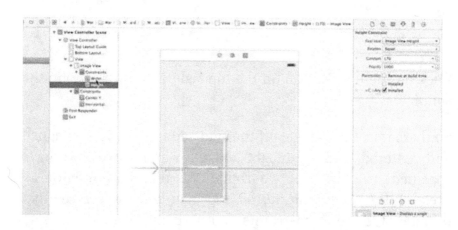

Now were going to add a second *imageview*. Let's go ahead and drag another *imageview* element representing the second card onto the interface builder in the center. Now, we want this card to be the same size as the first one. There's an easy way to do that; select the first card on the *project file navigator* pane on the left and then hold down *command* and select the second card. Now go down to the *Pin* option at the bottom and make sure to put a check on the *Equal Widths* and *Equal Heights* option and then click *Add 2 constraints*. Since we have already specified a widths and heights value for the first *imageview*, the second imageview is going to take the same constraints as well.

You can see right away on the project file navigator pane on the left that constraint entries have been added for the second *imageview*. Once you update frames, you will now see that both *imageviews* have the same dimensions.

Again, this second *imageview* won't have any positioning rules, that's why it is just all over the place. So we're going to click our second card image, then we're going to put a *Vertical Center in Container* constraint and update the frames.

You can see now that it is vertically centered. Then we're going to add another constraint and make it 50 pixels off the right side and update the frames again. Now you can see that they're more of a mirror to each other.

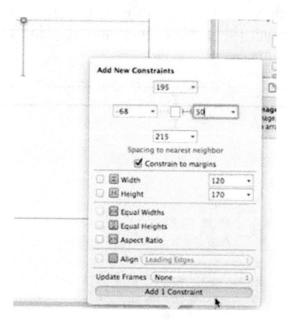

Let's again put a color so we can see it when we run it on the simulator by going to our color picker and selecting any color.

Now you can see that they're both vertically centered, they're both the same height and width and they're both 50 pixels from the edges. If you rotate it, the constraints keep it together.

Now at this point, if this is not what you see and this is not how you're app behaves, stop the simulator and what you can do is you can actually delete your constraints from the project file navigator pane and try again. Sometimes it can be a little finicky like that and it takes a little bit of practice.

What you could also do is you can select you element and you can go to *Resolve Auto Layout* at the bottom and click on *Clear constraints,* to wipe out all constraints for that element.

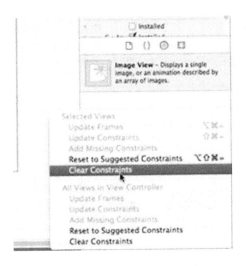

If you noticed when running the app in the simulator, in the landscape view the cards are very far apart and they're basically stuck on the edges of the left and right side with a very large white gap in the center. We want them to be kind of closer together like when you're viewing it in portrait mode. What you can do is highlight both elements and you can go up to the editor menu and click on *Pin → Horizontal spacing*. What that does is it adds a constraint that says that they must always be at a specific distance from each other all of the time.

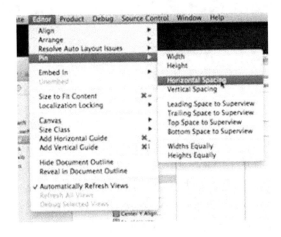

When you look at your *project file navigator* pane you will see the *Horizontal spacing* entry and if you look at the attributes on the right side it will have a constant value of 28.

Run it now on the simulator and this time you will see that they are keeping themselves at the same distance from each other in addition to keeping themselves 50 pixels from the edges as well.

But, again this is not what we are expecting. As you can see when you switch from portrait to landscape view, the cards stretches horizontally and doesn't keep the same card aspect ratio as when it is on portrait view.

You would also notice down at our Xcode debug area at the bottom, it says *"Unable to simultaneously satisfy constraints. Probably at least one of the constraints in the following list is one you don't want."*

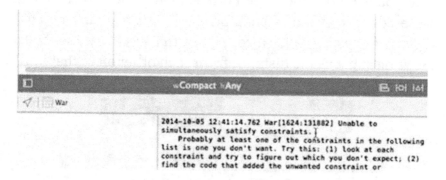

Let's take a look at why we're getting this error message and why we're getting this behavior. We added a new constraint to say that it should always be 28 pixels side by side, that they should be the same width and that they should be 50 pixels from the edges. But, there's one constraint that's actually conflicting with all of these constraints right now.

We have a constraint here that specifies that the Width should be equal to 120. While this constraint works well in portrait view, the width actually cannot be equal to 120 if we want it to be 50 pixels from the edges and we want it to be 28 pixels apart side by side in landscape view. It can't simultaneously satisfy all of those conditions together. At this point, it just didn't follow the Width constraint of 120 and instead just followed the 50 pixel from the edges and 28 pixels apart constraints.

To eliminate this behavior, what we're going to do is put the cards in another container and horizontally center that container. Go to your library pane at the lower right-hand side and type *uiview* in the search box and drag the *View* element to your interface editor. Select the two imageviews for the two cards and drag it into the new View element that we just created.

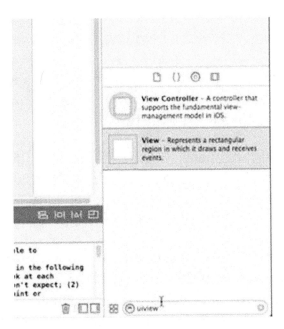

As you can see now on your project file navigator pane in the hierarchy of files, your two card *imageviews* are now under the new *View* that we added. Put a color on the new container view as well. Go to the Pin option below and let's give it a Width value of 280 and a Height value of 170. Make sure *Constraint to margins* option is also checked, and then click *Add 2 constraints* and update the frames.

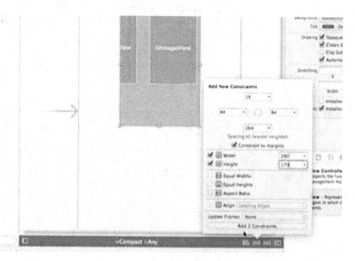

We also want to align it to the center, so let's add a *Vertical Center in Container* and *Horizontal Center in Container* constraints and then update the frames.

However, what happened when we added the two card imageviews into it is that they lost all of their constraints. If you look at the project file navigator pane, it lost all alignment constraints except the aspect ratio constraints for the cards.

So, we have to add new constraints to those card *imageviews* relative to the new container view that they are in now. So for the first card *imageview* let's pin it to the left and to the top by clicking the corresponding pin bars then click Add 2 constraints. For the second card view pin it to the top and right with zero margin value on the right and update your frames.

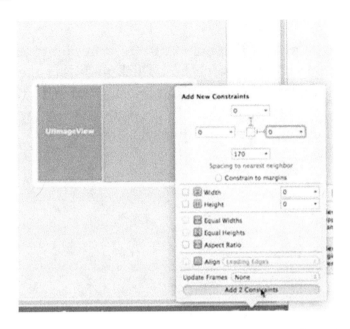

Another thing that we lost was that the second card image should be the same height and width as the first card image so select them both and go to pin and select the *Equal Widths* and *Equal Heights* options and click *Add 2 constraints* and update your frames.

So now, your second card imageview is equal in height and width and they both have the same positioning constraints aligning them to the top left and top right of the card container view with zero margin.

Now run your app on the simulator and see the results. Now as you can see both cards retain their constraints regardless of whether it is on portrait view or landscape view.

For the card container view, change it back to a transparent background. We mainly wanted a colored background to see where it was during testing.

Now were going to add a button. Go to your library pane and type "button" on the search box. Click and drag the Button element into your interface editor just below the two card imageviews. This button element is going to allow you to create something a user can tap to trigger something.

Go to your project file navigator pane on the left and rename your button to "PlayRoundButton". Double-click your button element on the interface navigator and rename it to "Play Round".

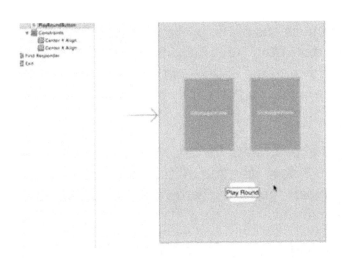

Now, in terms of alignment, we want to align it horizontally, so let's give it a *Horizontal Center in Container* constraint by checking that option and then click on *Add 1 constraint* and update your frames.

We also need to align it vertically, so let's anchor our *Play Round* button to the bottom by dragging it under the two card imageviews. Go to the pin options below, click on the pin bar for the bottom, and give it a margin value of 30 pixels. Make sure that the *Constrain to margins* option is checked, and then click *Add 1 constraint*. Update your frames and run the app on the simulator.

As you can see, the app looks decent in the landscape view. But, in the portrait view, we'd rather have it vertically centered between the bottom edge of the two card imageviews and the bottom edge of the interface editor itself.

We can achieve that the same way we did with the two card imageviews where we put them inside another container. So go to your library pane, type *uiview* on the search box, and click and drag the *View* element onto the interface builder.

47

Adjust the dimensions of the new container so that it takes up the whole area from the bottom edge of the two card imageviews down to the bottom of the interface builder. Go to your attributes pane and give it a color for now so you're able to see it.

We'll also add constraints for this view container by going to the Pin menu below, and add all four constraints by clicking on all the pin bars, and put a zero value for the top, left, right, and bottom margins.

Some of you might wonder, if you put a zero value on the top margin, wouldn't that topmost part of the view container anchor to the very top of the interface builder? Well, if you notice the text written just below the bottom margin box, it says "Spacing to nearest neighbor". The nearest neighbor to the view container is the card container view so when you update your frames it'll anchor to the bottom part of that.

Next we have to put the Play Round button inside the View container that we just made. You can accomplish this by going to your *project file navigator* pane on the left and just click and drag your PlayRound button file onto the new view container file. As soon as you do that, you will see that the PlayRound button file will be under the new container file and will be indented; an indication that the PlayRound file is under the new container view file.

Another thing to note is that after you move the PlayRound button inside the view container, it'll lose all of its constraints so just reapply them again and then change back the color of the view container back to transparent.

Run your app in the simulator. As you can see, in the portrait view and landscape view, the button looks better and it's positioned well.

The last thing we're going to do is add an image view for the background, since having a nice background for the entire game is essential. Go to your library pane and type "imageview" in the search box, and click and drag the Image view element onto the interface builder. Adjust the aspect ratio of the element to cover the whole area of the interface builder. Go ahead and click on the *Pin* option below and pin it to all four sides, making sure that all of the margin values are zero. This time, make sure that the *Constraint to margins* options is unchecked, click on *Add 4 Constraints*.

Also, add a background color for this just so you can see it when you run it in the simulator. Run your app in simulator. As you can see, it covers all elements that we have put in the interface builder before. We can adjust that by going to our project navigator pane again and making sure to move the Background image view file above the two-card container view and Play button container view element files.

So just like that you have created a user interface that conforms to both orientations, portrait and landscape, beautifully. That's why *Auto Layout* is very powerful considering the different display resolutions that are coming out. If it's your first time working with *Auto layout* it can be very frustrating and you may be adding and removing constraints and trying to get your UI elements positioned correctly and looking correct in both orientations. However, once you get the hang of it and you're familiar with how the constraints work and how they work in conjunction with each other, you won't have that pain anymore and you'll be able to harness the power of *Auto Layout* and create really adaptive layouts for any screen size.

Chapter 7:
Essential Swift Programming Concepts

In the last chapter, you built your user interface in the storyboard and you learned about Auto layout. Before we expose those elements to code, let's go through the basic building blocks of the Swift programming language so that when you do look at code, you can understand what is going on and what the various lines of code mean.

We're going to go over some concepts that may be difficult for you to understand if this is the first time you have ever seen or heard about them. We're going to go over three concepts mainly:

1. Classes & Objects

2. Methods

3. Properties

The Swift Class

The first concept is the Class. A Class is a blueprint that we can create to describe a component of your app. When you're making an app in Xcode, really all you're doing is creating classes to describe the various components of your app and how they interact with each other.

For example, in the MVC (Model View Controller) diagram that we discussed before describing the various components of an app, the behavior of the model will be described by a class, the View Controller is described by a class and the View as well. In each of these classes we write code to give it instructions on what to do and how to act. So, in the view

51

controller class, you might write some code to tell it to ask the model for the data and then display it to the view. In the model class, we might write some code to say if the view controller asks you for some data then go fetch the data and then return it.

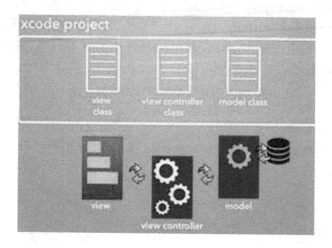

So a class contains instructions written in code to describe how a component is supposed to act and how it's supposed to interact with the other components. Another thing to realize is that it's not the classes themselves that are doing the interacting; the classes are merely blueprints that we are creating. What happens is that these blueprints, also known as classes, are turned into what's called objects. So, from the model class, a model object is created. From the view controller class, a view controller object is created. From the view class, a view object is created.

These objects are the ones that interact with each other and carry out the functions of your app. Furthermore, from one class or blueprint, you can create multiples objects in the same likeness and behavior that the class describes. This makes sense because if you had two components in your app that did the same thing but in two different places, you can code up one class and create two objects from it.

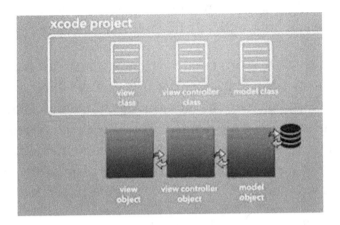

Another example would be in a game where you spawn multiples enemies of the same type. You shouldn't need to create a class for each enemy that appears on the screen. You only need to create a single class that describes the enemy's behavior and use that class to create multiple enemy objects to throw at the player.

So the key takeaways at this point are the following:

1. Components in our app are described by classes.

2. Classes are like blueprints and are used to produce objects that behave as instructed in the class.

3. These objects interact with each other to perform the functionality of your app.

Now let's try creating some classes on the playground in Xcode just like what we discussed in Chapter 2. So to create a class, simply use the class keyword and then give your class a name. For example, we're going to call our class Person, and then all you're going to do is open up a set of curly braces.

Inside the curly braces, you're going to type *init* then an open and close parenthesis and then another set of curly braces. So, when you type a set of curly braces, as soon as you type first one, Xcode will automatically fill-in the second one.

So just like that, you created a new class to describe a component of your app. So what is this *init*? Well, any code that you put in between the curly braces immediately after *init* gets executed when a new object of this class gets created. So when a new Person object is created, the code inside the *init* is run and that code can be used to setup or initialize anything that you need for the Person object to function properly.

So let's try to create a new object of our new Person class. You can do that very simply just by typing the class name followed by an open and close parenthesis.

Just like that, we have created a new object. However, what we want to do is create a variable just so that we can reference our new object later. So let's create a new variable named "a".

```
// Playground - noun: a place where people can play

import UIKit

var str = "Hello, playground"                    "Hello, playground"

class Person {

    init () {

    }

}

Person()                                          Person

var a = Person()                                  Person
```

So now we've created a new *Person* object and assigned it to the variable *a*. So now when we want to reference that object, we can use the variable *a*. Let's try to put a *println* statement in the *init* just so we can see what it gets called when we create a new object.

Now, when you create a new *Person* object, you can see that the *println* statement is executed and you can see the output.

So we've created a new class to describe a component in our app, but we need to give it instructions to do something or to describe its behavior. How do we do that? We do that through something called Methods and Properties. Let's talk about Methods first.

The Swift Method

A Method is a named set of instructions that will be executed when called. Additionally, Methods can accept some data as input and return some data as output back to the caller of the method. Finally, Methods are associated with a class.

So let's try to create a method for your new Person class. In order to create a method, you start with the func keyword, and you give your Method a name. Let's call it "sayCheese" in this instance, followed by a set of parenthesis and immediately followed by a set of curly braces. Inside this set of curly braces, you write the code to execute when this method is called.

So inside of the *sayCheese* method we're going to put the code *println ("Cheese")*. As you can see, when we created a new object with the line of code var b = Person (), "Cheese" doesn't get printed out because the println ("Cheese") line of code only gets executed if the func *sayCheese* method is called.

What you can do to call the method, considering that we made a new Person object assigned to the variable "b", is just type *b.sayCheese()*. When you do that, you can see in the output pane that it prints the word "Cheese" as indicated in the line of code *println("Cheese")*.

So when we write the code statement *b.sayCheese()* it actually runs the code *println("Cheese")*. Let's look at the method call b.sayCheese(). What is b.sayCheese()? Well, Method calls take the format of the object that you want to call the method on followed by a "." then the method name.

```
// Playground - noun: a place where people can play

import UIKit

var str = "Hello, playground"                              Hello, playground

class Person {

    init () {
        println("New person initialized")                  New person initialized
    }

    func sayCheese () {
        println("Cheese")                                  Cheese
    }

}

var b = Person()                                           Person

b.sayCheese()                                              Person
```

So that's why because our person object is in the variable "b", when we write *b*, that refers to that object. We then write "."after *b* to look at its properties and methods. At this point it only has the sayCheese method, and then you write the method name to call the *b* object *sayCheese* method.

Let's say we don't do that. Instead, let's try to call that method as part of the initializer. You might notice at this point that this initializer kind of looks like a method except that it doesn't have the func keyword. You're actually right, the initializer is basically a method, but it's a special type of method because all classes need to have an initializer.

So, let's erase the *println* code under *init* and instead we're going to call the *sayCheese* method from inside *init*, so that whenever we create a new *Person* object, this initializer method is run and inside this *init* method, it will call its own *sayCheese* method.

The way we do that is we write *self.sayCheese()*. As you can see, when we create a new Person object and assign it to var b, "Cheese" is printed out even though we didn't call the method explicitly. This is because the init method calls the sayCheese method.

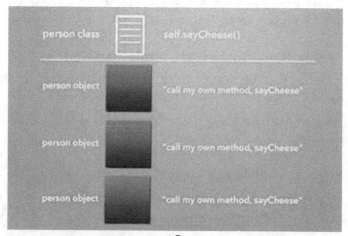

```
                    MyPlayground.playground — Edited
      MyPlayground.playground > No Selection
1   // Playground - noun: a place where people can play
2
3   import UIKit
4
5   var str = "Hello, playground"                        "Hello, playground"
6
7   class Person {
8
9       init () {
10          self.sayCheese()
11      }
12
13      func sayCheese () {
14          println("Cheese")                             "Cheese"
15      }
16
17  }
18
19  var b = Person()                                      Person
20
21  |     I
```

Now you might be wondering, what is this "*self*" keyword we used? *Self* means call a method that you own yourself. Imagine that we're writing a set of instructions for the created object to read itself. Each object is created in the likeness of the class and when they read that line of code, they are like saying to themselves, call my own method *sayCheese*. If you think about it that way, it may be more intuitive to understand why the keyword is named *self*.

The Swift Property

A property is something we can create for a class in order to allow it to store a value or keep track of another object. Open up your Xcode Playground and let's see how to declare a property for your class.

Properties are always declared at the very top within the class. Start with the keyword var followed by the property name, followed by a ":", followed by the type of data that the property is going to store or trap. In this case, let's type the keyword String. Remember that a String is a piece of text. Next we're going to designate an initial value so let's use the "=" symbol and assign "Initial Name" as the piece of text.

So just like that we've declared a property for your person class and gave it an initial value. You may notice that a property declaration almost looks like a variable declaration. If you remember in Chapter 2 when we did something like the ones below:

```
// Playground - noun: a place where people can play

import UIKit

var str = "Hello, playground"          Hello, playground

class Person {

    var Name:String = "Initial Name"

    init () {
        self.sayCheese()
    }

    func sayCheese () {
        println("Cheese")
    }

}

var a = 10                              10
var b = 15                              15
var total = a + b                       25
```

This almost looks like a property declaration. You have the var keyword and you a name for your variable. You're right because even with the variable declaration, we can put a colon and the type of data that the variable is going to hold. For example, Int which stands for integer.

```
// Playground - noun: a place where people can play

import UIKit

var str = "Hello, playground"          Hello, playground

class Person {

    var Name:String = "Initial Name"

    init () {
        self.sayCheese()
    }

    func sayCheese () {
        println("Cheese")
    }

}

var a:Int = 10                          10
var b:Int = 15                          15
var total:Int = a + b                   25
```

So, we could have done this. Now it looks more like a property declaration. In fact, it's actually a good practice if you know the type of data that variable is going to be tracking, so you

60

don't accidentally use that variable later expecting a number but maybe you accidentally get another type in there thus creating a bug that you may even not know about. By specifying the type that you expect to be in there, if you try to put another type of data in that variable, it will complain and it won't let you.

So what are the differences between variables and properties? Well, it depends where it is declared. When it's declared inside a class, it becomes a property of that class and it is associated with that class. Variables, however, are declared and used within methods.

Variables are normally declared within methods, but since we're just working on the Xcode Playground where this is just a place to test code, that rule is not applied here. But, you'll notice whenever you write code inside Xcode itself, you will be following those rules where most of the variables that you declare will be inside methods and anything that we declare outside are properties.

So let's create a variable called *firstPerson* and then create a new *Person* object. In order to access that property, it follows the same format as a method call, we reference the object that we want to call its property on, put a "." and then now we can either write *sayCheese()* to call its method or write the property name to call its property.

As you can see on the output window its accessed Initial Name. Now if you want to change the property, you can just type *firstPerson.Name* = *"Alice"* where we assign it a different piece of text. Now if we access that property again, you can see that it has changed and now it says *Alice*.

Let's create a second variable and create a new person, assign it to that second variable and we're going to change its name property.

```
class Person {

    var Name:String = "Initial Name"

    init () {
        self.sayCheese()
    }

    func sayCheese () {                        (2 times)
        println("Cheese")
    }

}

var firstPerson = Person()                     {Name "Initial Name"}

firstPerson.Name                               "Initial Name"
firstPerson.Name = "Alice"                     {Name "Alice"}
firstPerson.Name                               "Alice"

var secondPerson = Person()                    {Name "Initial Name"}

secondPerson.Name = "Bob"                      {Name "Bob"}
```

Let's take a closer look at this. We've created another person object, assigned it to the variable secondPerson and we just changed its name to Bob. So what do you think the variable firstPerson name would be? As you can see, the name is still Alice. This illustrates a very important point about objects; which is although each object is created in the likeness of the class, they are actually independent instances of each other. Remember, you can use one class to create multiple objects of that class, but each of them are independent instances. So what you do to one object doesn't actually apply to all objects, they're independent.

If this was your first time learning about classes and objects, then welcome to the world of object oriented programming languages. You'll probably need to go over this chapter a few more times to wrap your head around it. Swift, along with many other programming languages are object oriented. So, in the future when you've mastered Swift and you decide to learn Java for Android apps, C# for windows phone apps or perhaps even Objective C, you'll have a head start because they use the same concepts that have been presented in this book.

Conclusion

Thank you again for downloading this book!

I hope this book was able to help you learn more about IOS programming!

The next step is to put this information to use and begin using IOS programming to create your very own apps for iPhone and iPad!

Finally, if you enjoyed this book, please take the time to share your thoughts and post a review on Amazon. It'd be greatly appreciated!

Thank you and good luck!

www.ingramcontent.com/pod-product-compliance
Lightning Source LLC
LaVergne TN
LVHW050149060326
832904LV00003B/71